I0159001

The 15-Second Rule for Overthinkers

ISBN: 979-8-9990664-1-1

Published by Amaury Almodovar Lugo

Printed in the United States

Disclaimer

This book is intended for informational and educational purposes only. The strategies and insights shared here are based on personal experience, research, and expert perspectives. The author and publisher are not responsible for any specific outcomes resulting from the application of these principles. Readers are encouraged to use their judgment and seek professional advice when making important decisions.

THE
15-SECOND
RULE
FOR OVERTHINKERS

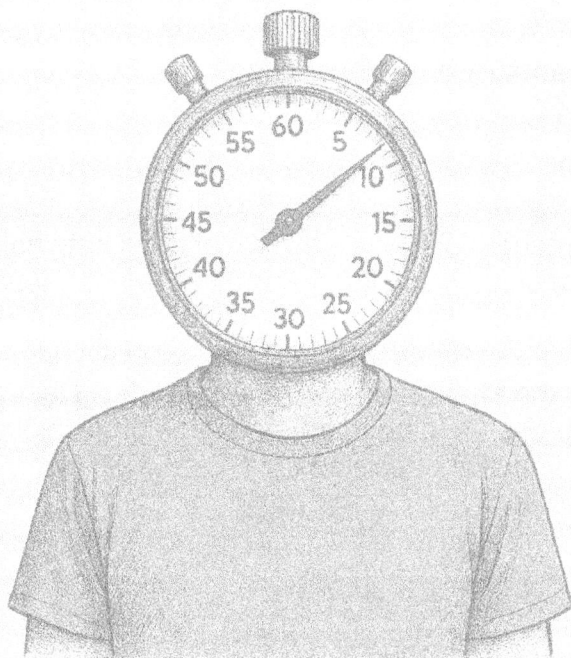

AMAURY ALMODOVAR LUGO

Dedicated to

To my dad, who taught me the value of having a strong moral compass.

To my mom, whose bravery and faith inspire us all.

To MJ, my soulmate, who never ceases to amaze me with her courage in every heartbeat and breath. Thank you for your unwavering belief in me.

To my son, we are inspired every day by your bravery and tenacity.

For all of you overthinkers, perfectionists, dreamers, and self-doubters!

Remember that you are not alone on this road.

I have been there, too!

I created this book as a guide for all who are just one decision away from realizing their full potential. May this help you embrace growth and set the pace for a new beginning without fear.

About the Designer // Author: Amaury Almodovar Lugo

Husband. Father. Brother. Son. Mentor.

Amaury was born in Puerto Rico to Vilma and Amaury and grew up in a small town on the island's west coast, surrounded by its vibrant culture and natural beauty.

As a parent, he recognized the importance of setting a good example for his son by venturing outside his comfort zone and demonstrating that anything is possible when you take chances and face the world head-on. Through hesitancy and doubt, he realized that developing the ability to make quick, confident decisions was a skill worth honing—not just for himself but also for those around him.

The Mission Behind This Book

Feeling stuck over a decision can be overwhelming and often prevents the world from experiencing the best version of you. I have fallen into the trap of overthinking more times than I can count, which has led to inaction. This inability to make decisions has crushed my hopes, slowed my progress, and caused persistent doubt.

Personal challenges and missed opportunities inspired Amaury to share what worked for him. The 15-second Rule is more than just a strategy; it is a mindset shift designed to help people regain control, trust their instincts, and move forward without fear.

Professional Experience

With over 20 years of experience in sales, people management, and mentoring, Amaury has interacted with people from diverse backgrounds and learned a universal truth: hesitation affects us all, regardless of our background, personality, or ambition.

Previous Works

The 15-Second Rule for Overthinkers is Amaury's first book, marking the beginning of his authorial journey dedicated to self-growth and empowerment.

Personal Journey

Being a parent drives you to take control, be brave, and act even when you do not feel ready. Overthinking can cloud judgment and possibilities, stall growth, and limit progress.

Both personally and professionally, the significance of agile thinking and effective problem-solving is often underestimated.

Amaury's goal is simple: to put something good into the world—to remind people that every win, every forward step, and every moment of courage is a victory worth celebrating.

Where to Connect

Stay inspired and follow Amaury's journey:

AMAURYALMODOVARLUGO

Table of Contents

Introduction

Introduction:

The Overthinking Trap

Often in life, we waste time overthinking, lingering on decisions far longer than necessary. We spent even more time wondering what it could have been if we had taken that first step. While thoughtful reflection is valuable in certain situations, excessive analysis can create unnecessary anxiety, often delay opportunities, and lead to inaction. The ability to think fast and decide efficiently can mean the difference between fulfilling your potential and staying stuck.

The 15-Second Rule is designed to end self-doubt and help you focus only on what you can control while letting go of what you cannot. This principle rewires your brain to process decisions instantly, replacing hesitation with clarity, confidence, and action.

By the time you finish this book, you will no longer be trapped in overanalysis. Instead, you will train yourself to assess situations quickly, make decisions within seconds, and trust the power of fast thinking to create better outcomes. Most importantly, you will learn to trust yourself and your instincts.

Chapter 1:

How Your Brain Processes Decisions

Two primary systems of thought influence your decision-making process, which translates into millions of messages that your brain processes from emotions, social cues, previous experiences, and future projections. According to neuroscience, these are the two primary systems of thought:

1. Quick Thinking (Automatic & Intuitive) ** - Your intuition, quick decisions, and agile reactions are all governed by this system.

It enables reflexive choices, such as answering a question or replying in a dialogue.

It is crucial for daily decision-making, social interaction, and ensuring your survival instincts are activated.

2. **Deliberate and Analytical Slow Thinking** - This system is responsible for long-term planning, sophisticated problem-solving, and logical thinking. It is what you use when confronted with difficult choices, such as monetary investments, commercial endeavors, or ethical quandaries. Although it requires deliberate effort, it may also unduly delay your responses.

Both cognitive systems play a crucial role; however, overthinkers tend to get stuck in System 2, analyzing every detail and second-guessing even the smallest decisions. The 15-Second Rule is designed to strengthen System 1 (quick thinking), helping you make faster, more confident choices in everyday situations while reserving System 2 for moments that truly require deeper thought.

Chapter 1:

First Exercise: Addressing Overthinking

The first step to making faster decisions is understanding when and why you hesitate. This exercise helps you recognize your patterns of overthinking, discover the reasons behind them, and create a plan to let go of the things that are not within your control. The more aware you become, the easier it is to move forward with confidence.

Step 1: Identify the Times You Overthink Things

Think back to three recent choices that were made more slowly than required. Write them down.

Examples include:

- Putting off responding to an email because you were preoccupied with making things "perfect."
- Excessive analysis of a buying choice.
- Being reluctant to express your thoughts during a discussion or meeting.

Step 2: Break Down the Cause

In each case, consider the following:

- For what reason did I hesitate? Was it a fear of uncertainty, perfectionism, or failure?
- What factors did I influence? Was there anything I could have done with the knowledge I had?
- What factors did I have no control over? Was my time wasted fretting about things I could not alter?

Chapter 1:

Step 3: Implement the 15-Second Rule

Choose one of the **three decisions** and challenge yourself to **make a similar decision in 15 seconds** next time.

- If it is an email, commit to starting your reply within 15 seconds, without overanalyzing the subject line.
- If it is a purchase, give yourself a firm deadline to decide based on your understanding.
- If it is a discussion, answer right away without censoring yourself needlessly.

Date			
Questions Attempted			
Time Taken (15 sec max)			
Did hesitation occur? (Yes/No)			
Confidence Level (1-10)			
Outcome & Insights			

Chapter 1:

Step 4: Monitor Your Advancement

Commit to this exercise every day for a week, then take a moment to evaluate your progress. How did it feel to make decisions more quickly? Did your hesitation start to fade? Push yourself, track your progress, and own the change!

Date			
Questions Attempted			
Time Taken (15 sec max)			
Did hesitation occur? (Yes/No)			
Confidence Level (1-10)			
Outcome & Insights			

Date			
Questions Attempted			
Time Taken (15 sec max)			
Did hesitation occur? (Yes/No)			
Confidence Level (1-10)			
Outcome & Insights			

Chapter 2:

Understanding the Brain—Why We Hesitate

Hesitation is not a personal flaw, but in reality, it is deeply rooted in how our brain processes information. When faced with a decision, your brain does what it is supposed to; it tries to predict outcomes, assess risks, and weigh options, all while balancing emotions and logic. This process can be helpful, but when overthinking takes over, it slows everything down, feeds our anxiety, creates stress, and leads us to a path to nowhere.

Why Overthinkers Struggle with Fast Decisions

Most overthinkers rely too much on System 2, obsessing over every detail excessively while ignoring their intuitive reactions. This action creates a loop where:

- They feel unsure → so they analyze more.
- More analysis leads to self-doubt.
- Self-doubt causes hesitation, further delaying the Decision.
- The delay fuels anxiety, making it even harder to decide.

The outcome of overanalyzing is mental fatigue, a decline in confidence, and making even simple decisions feel overwhelming. Breaking this pattern requires shifting from System 2 to System 1 in everyday situations; using structured techniques, such as the 15-Second Rule, leads to making choices efficiently and confidently.

Chapter 2:

Exercise 2: Thought Sorting

This Exercise helps you identify when System 2 is overcomplicating a decision and teaches you to filter out unnecessary details.

Step 1: Choose a Recent Decision

Write down a choice that took too long to make. Examples might include:

- ✓ Deciding whether to attend an event
- ✓ Struggling to choose between two similar products
- ✓ Debating how to respond to someone in a conversation.

Decision:

_____
_____
_____
_____
_____
_____
_____
_____
_____
_____
_____
_____

Chapter 2:

Step 2: Categorize Your Thoughts

Break the Decision into two categories:

- What was within your control? (Facts, resources, actions you could take)
- What was NOT within your control? (External opinions, future uncertainties, hypothetical scenarios)

Date			
What was within your control?			
What was NOT within your control?			

Date			
What was within your control?			
What was NOT within your control?			

Chapter 2:

Step 3: End Unnecessary Overthinking

Focus ONLY on the factors you control and set a 15-second decision window.

Remove thoughts about things you cannot change—they add nothing but hesitation.

Final Decision made within 15 seconds:

Step 4: Practice Fast Thinking

For the following three small decisions, give yourself 15 seconds to decide using only relevant information.

Decision	Time Taken	Did hesitation reduce?	Outcome & Lessons Learned

Chapter 2:

By training your brain to move away from unnecessary analysis, you free up mental space and gain confidence in your decision-making.

Shifting from System 2 Back to System 1 in High-Pressure Moments

- Overthinkers often become trapped in System 2 thinking, particularly in high-stakes situations, such as negotiations, interviews, public speaking, or even everyday social interactions. Instead of reacting instinctively, they stall, overanalyze, and hesitate, losing control of the conversation or opportunity.

- The key to thinking faster under pressure is learning to rely on System 1 when needed. You do not need to process every single detail before deciding—you need to focus on what matters most at that moment.

The 3-Step Process to React Instantly

When faced with a high-pressure decision, use this method to switch back to fast-thinking mode:

Step 1: Recognize the Overthinking Cycle (5 Seconds)

- If you notice hesitation creeping in, stop and take a moment to reset.
- Ask yourself: Am I making this Decision harder than it needs to be?
- Identify what is essential right now and ignore what's irrelevant.

Chapter 2:

Step 2: Default to a Rapid Response Framework (10 Seconds)

Choose one of these instant decision strategies, depending on the situation:

- The Gut Rule: If your first instinct feels right, trust it and act.
- The 80/20 Rule: Focus on the most critical 20% of information to decide.
- The Past-Experience Rule: Recall a similar situation and apply that decision pattern.

Step 3: Commit & Execute Without Pausing (Final 15 Seconds)

- Once you decide, act without second-guessing.
- Say your answer aloud, press send on the email, make the call—just move forward.
- If needed, adjust later, but don't stay stuck in hesitation.

Exercise 3: Speed Response Drill

This Exercise builds instant decision-making reflexes by training your brain to process information rapidly.

Chapter 2:

Fast Thinking Challenge: Overcoming Hesitation

Step 1: Pick Five Questions

Choose five situations where hesitation would typically occur. Write them down below:

Step 2: Set 15 Seconds on your clock

☑ Answer each question quickly and instinctively—write it down or say it aloud.

☑ Do not overthink—trust your first reaction.

Chapter 2:

Step 3: Repeat Daily & Increase Difficulty

Each day, increase the challenge by:

✓ Picking new questions that push your comfort zone.

✓ Observing how your responses become sharper and more confident over time.

✓ Recognizing the decline in hesitation as fast thinking becomes second nature.

Mastering this method ensures you never freeze under pressure again—your brain will default to immediate action, cutting hesitation before it starts.

Chapter 3:

Breaking Time into Strategic Intervals

The 15-Second Rule is a method designed to train your brain to process information faster. Breaking Time into Strategic Intervals sets the pace for your fast decision-making journey to begin. This enables you to make confident decisions in real-time. Instead of getting stuck in overthinking, you learn to break time into four distinct intervals, each serving a specific function to keep decisions clear, efficient, and actionable.

This approach ensures that every minute is optimized, allowing you to think, decide, and act within structured time blocks.

Let the training begin!

- Every decision you make can be broken into four 15-second intervals, creating a structured process for faster thinking.

Step 1: Observe (First 15 Seconds)

✓ Take in the situation without overcomplicating it.

✓ Identify only the key details that matter for the Decision.

✓ Filter out distractions, unnecessary details, and emotional hesitation.

Step 2: Analyze (Second 15 Seconds)

✓ Focus only on what you can control—ignore external factors.

✓ Quickly weigh possible actions without overthinking.

✓ Rely on past experiences or gut reactions to guide you.

Chapter 3:

Step 3: Decide (Third 15 Seconds)

✓ Commit to an immediate course of action—no hesitation.

✓ Eliminate unnecessary second-guessing.

✓ Frame your choice in clear, confident terms to reinforce it.

Step 4: Execute (Final 15 Seconds)

✓ Act, make the call, send the email, say the words.

✓ Reinforce the Decision with assertiveness and control.

✓ Move forward without doubting or revisiting the choice.

How the Rule Maximizes Every Interaction

This structured 15-second cycle applies to any decision—from conversations to professional choices to personal habits. Here's how it transforms everyday moments:

Negotiations & Sales: Quickly assess the other person's intent, analyze their objections, decide on your response, and execute confidently.

Daily Conversations: React to tough questions, witty remarks, or meaningful discussions without hesitating.

Personal Choices: Make faster, stress-free decisions about where to go, what to buy, and how to respond in demanding situations.

Chapter 3:

By repeating this framework, your brain learns to process decisions efficiently until it becomes second nature.

Exercise 4: Rapid Fire Decision-Making

This exercise strengthens mental agility by training your brain to think quickly and commit to action within 15-second intervals.

Step 1: Choose Three Past Decisions

- ✓ Pick three situations where overthinking delays action. Examples might include:
    - o Hesitating before responding to someone in conversation.
    - o Struggling to choose between two business opportunities.
    - o Avoiding a decision out of fear of choosing incorrectly.

Step 2: Replay Those Scenarios Using the 15-second Rule

Imagine reliving those moments, but this time, force your brain to make a quick decision.

Break the thought process into four 15-second intervals:

✓ Observe the situation.

✓ Analyze only what matters.

✓ Decide on the best immediate action.

✓ Execute without hesitation.

Chapter 3:

Step 3: Apply the Rule in Real Time

Choose three new decisions today and apply the structured 15-second cycle to train fast thinking.

Track results to see how speed improves decision-making confidence.

Decisions	Observe	Analyze	Decide	Execute

Final Thought

The 15-Second Rule is a mental discipline that teaches your brain to prioritize action over hesitation. The more you train yourself to think quickly, the easier it becomes to control decisions, navigate challenges, and eliminate second-guessing.

Chapter 4:

Practical Exercises to Train Fast Thinking:

The brain can be trained and developed. Just like athletes strengthen reflexes through repetition, you can sharpen mental agility using targeted exercises designed to eliminate hesitation and improve rapid response ability. Fast decision-making isn't just a skill.

This chapter provides structured drills to rewire your brain for faster, more confident thinking in everyday situations.

Exercise 1: Writing Speed Drill

✦ Goal: Train your brain to process thoughts quickly without overanalyzing.

Step 1: Set Up Your Timer

- ✓ Grab a notebook, open a writing app, or open a blank document.
- ✓ Write down a random topic (e.g., "How would I describe my dream job?").
- ✓ Set a 15-second countdown.

Step 2: Write Without Stopping

- ✓ Start writing at once; don't pause for corrections or second-guessing.
- ✓ Ignore grammar, structure, or perfection—just keep going until time runs out.

Step 3: Repeat & Adjust

- ✓ Repeat with different topics every day.
- ✓ Over time, notice how your thoughts flow faster without hesitation

Chapter 4:

✓ ⚡ Why It Works: This drill forces your brain to prioritize action over overthinking, strengthening your ability to think and respond instantly.

Chapter 4:

Exercise 2: Verbal Speed Response Drill

◆ Goal: Improve fast verbal thinking and eliminate hesitation in conversations.

Step 1: Choose a Prompt

- ✓ Pick a question that would generally make you pause (e.g., "What's your biggest strength?").
- ✓ Set a 15-second countdown before answering.

Step 2: Speak Without Stopping

- ✓ Answer at once—no hesitation, no filtering.
- ✓ Keep talking until time runs out, even if you ramble.

Step 3: Reflect & Repeat

- ✓ Repeat daily with different questions.
- ✓ Gradually refine answers while keeping speed.

Why It Works: This strengthens mental reflexes, helping you stay confident and articulate even in high-pressure moments.

Chapter 4:

Exercise 3: Rapid Decision Challenge

✦ Goal: Train your ability to decide quickly under real-time constraints.

Step 1: Set Up Small Daily Decisions

- ✓ Pick three daily choices that typically take you too long to decide (e.g., what to eat, what email to send first).

Step 2: Apply the 15-Second Rule

- ✓ Observe → Analyze → Decide → Execute, within a strict 15-second window.
- ✓ Stick to your choice—no second-guessing or changing your mind later.

Step 3: Track Your Progress

- ✓ Journal how fast decisions change your stress levels over time.
- ✓ Look for patterns where hesitation is used to hold you back.

Why It Works: Because you train yourself to trust your instincts and act immediately.

Final Thought: Training Fast Thinking Like a Reflex

Just like a muscle learns movement through repetition and real-world application, these exercises reprogram hesitation, ensuring that when faced with an opportunity or challenge, you react decisively without fear or doubt.

Chapter 5:

Everyday Applications for Quick Thinking

Fast decision-making is a valuable life skill that can significantly enhance your ability to navigate conversations, negotiations, and daily challenges. When done correctly, the 15-Second Rule gives you an advantage in social interactions, business decisions, and even personal growth.

This chapter will break down how fast thinking improves three key areas of life:

✓ Social Confidence → Reacting quickly in conversations, debates, and unexpected situations.

✓ Business & Career → Handling negotiations, problem-solving, and leadership decisions with precision.

✓ Personal Growth → Reducing stress, eliminating hesitation, and trusting instincts.

Chapter 5:

1. Social Interactions: Sharpening Conversational Reflexes

Ever struggled to think of a comeback or a smooth response in a conversation?

Overthinkers often hesitate before speaking, analyzing every outcome before responding. The 15-Second Rule trains you to react instantly and keep conversations flowing naturally.

Applying Quick Thinking in Social Settings

✓ Use the four-step interval to listen, analyze, respond, and reinforce.

✓ Avoid hesitation—trust your first instinct and speak confidently.

✓ If stuck, use a response you've successfully used before in a similar setting.

◆ Exercise:

Pick a common conversation scenario (e.g., someone asks, "What do you do?").

Set a 15-second timer and practice answering without hesitation.

Repeat daily with different social questions to strengthen reflexes.

Chapter 5:

2. Business & Career: Negotiating & Leading with Speed

🏆 Successful professionals think fast and make decisive moves. Whether pitching a product, responding in a meeting, or managing a tough negotiation, quick thinking builds confidence and authority.

How to Use the 15-Second Rule in Business

✓ In negotiations, respond immediately to objections—don't give hesitation room to grow; this weakens your position.

✓ When problem-solving, apply the 4 intervals, observe → Analyze → Decide → Execute, before acting.

✓ Use fast thinking to control the pace of conversations, keeping others engaged and responsive.

◆ Exercise:

Choose a business challenge or Decision (e.g., responding to a client's objection).

Set a 15-second timer and craft a clear, concise response.

Repeat with different scenarios to build instant negotiation confidence.

3. Personal Growth: Breaking Hesitation & Reducing Stress

💬 Indecision creates stress—action eliminates it. The more quickly you make decisions, the less mental energy you waste on doubt. Fast thinking allows you to trust your instincts and focus on growth.

Applying Quick Decision-Making in Daily Life

✓ Apply the Rule in everyday decisions (e.g., where to eat, which project to tackle first).

Chapter 5:

✓ Use real-time decision tracking—write down choices that took too long and train yourself to make them faster next time.

✓ Shift mindset from hesitation → action, removing stress by cutting mental clutter.

◆ Exercise:

Identify three daily decisions that take too long.

Apply the 15-Second Rule—force yourself to decide and act immediately.

Repeat for a week, analyzing how speed improves confidence and clarity.

Date			
Decisions			
Time Taken (15 sec max)			
Did hesitation occur? (Yes/No)			
Confidence Level (1-10)			
Outcome & Insights			

Final Thought: Making Fast Thinking Second Nature

The 15-Second Rule isn't just a trick—it's a transformational mindset. When applied consistently, it turns hesitation into decisiveness, uncertainty into confidence, and slow responses into sharp reflexes

Chapter 6:

Breaking the Cycle of Hesitation

Hesitation isn't just a habit; it's a conditioned response that keeps you stuck in over-analysis, fear, and doubt. The more you overthink, the harder it becomes to make agile, confident decisions. Breaking the cycle requires conscious rewiring, which shifts your mindset from hesitation to action.

In this chapter, we'll explore:

✓ Why hesitation happens and how it affects decision-making.

✓ The psychological trick to interrupt doubt instantly.

✓ A structured method to regain control of your choices.

Why Hesitation Happens

Every time you delay a decision; your brain reacts to uncertainty and fear of failure. Overthinkers often hesitate because they:

- ✓ Want to avoid making the wrong choice?
- ✓ I feel overwhelmed by too many options.
- ✓ Get caught up in overanalyzing small details.
- ✓ Worry about what others will think.

The problem? Hesitation feeds self-doubt.

Chapter 6:

The 15-Second Interruption Method

To break hesitation permanently, use this four-step interruption method whenever you feel stuck in over-analysis:

Step 1: Recognize Hesitation in Real Time (First 15 Seconds)

- ✓ Whenever you catch yourself stuck, pause and identify the hesitation that's holding you back.
- ✓ Ask: What's holding me back from deciding right now?
- ✓ Separate fear-based hesitation from logical thinking.

Step 2: Shift Focus to What You Can Control (Second 15 Seconds)

- ✓ Pinpoint only the factors within your control—ignore distractions.
- ✓ Simplify the choice by removing unnecessary details.
- ✓ Reframe hesitation into an action statement:
- ✓ Instead of "I don't know what to do," say, "I will choose based on what I know now."

Step 3: Commit to an Immediate Decision (Third 15 Seconds)

- ✓ Make a firm choice without second-guessing.
- ✓ Use the 80/20 rule—focus on the most critical 20% of information to decide.
- ✓ Say your Decision aloud—it reinforces commitment.

Step 4: Execute Without Looking Back (Final 15 Seconds)

- ✓ Act immediately, send the message, say the words, and move forward.
- ✓ Avoid rethinking or revisiting—the Decision is done.
- ✓ If needed, adjust later, but never hesitate in the moment.

Chapter 6:

Exercise 6: Mental Reset Countdown

This Exercise trains your brain to override hesitation with immediate action.

Step 1: Identify One Decision You've Been Hesitating On

- ✓ Picking something you've been overthinking for too long can be small (a response to an email) or big (a business decision).

Step 2: Apply the Mental Reset Countdown

Use this structured four-step countdown to interrupt hesitation:

1. First 15 Seconds: Acknowledge hesitation and reframe your mindset.

2. Second 15 Seconds: Identify only the controllable elements.

3. Third 15 Seconds: Choose a firm action—commit mentally.

4. Final 15 Seconds: Execute immediately—send the message, make the call, and move forward.

Step 3: Track Your Results

- ✓ Repeat daily for a week, applying the reset method to different situations.
- ✓ Measure how your hesitation decreases over time.

Final Thought: Turn Hesitation into Action

Breaking hesitation isn't about removing uncertainty entirely—it's about learning to act despite it. The more you practice interrupting doubt and making fast decisions, the more confident you become in trusting your instincts and moving forward

Chapter 7:

Success Stories

Objective: Demonstrate how mastering fast decision-making has led to success in all walks of life, anywhere from businesses, entrepreneurship and personal growth. This chapter provides concrete examples, supported by psychological and business studies, to inspire readers to trust their instincts and take decisive action.

The Science Behind Rapid Decision-Making

Making decisions quickly under pressure has been widely studied in cognitive psychology and behavioral economics. Research from institutions like the Harvard Business Review and the Journal of Behavioral Decision-Making shows that:

Making quick decisions reduces stress and boosts confidence, thereby minimizing the likelihood of regret.

Overthinking can lead to decision paralysis, making people less effective in both their business and personal lives.

Gut-based decisions often prove more accurate because they rely on years of subconscious experience rather than forced rationalization.

Chapter 7:

Section 1:

Business Leaders & Entrepreneurs – The Power of Quick Thinking

Richard Branson – The Instinctive Risk-Taker

Richard Branson's business empire was built on rapid decision-making. Whether launching Virgin Atlantic on a whim or expanding into new industries, Branson credits his success to trusting his instincts and acting swiftly.

📖 Case Study: Decision-Making in Business Growth

🔍 Source: FasterCapital

A study on successful entrepreneurs reveals that hesitation can lead to missed opportunities, while decisive action fosters business expansion.

💡 Key Takeaway: The ability to make decisions in seconds, not hours, can propel businesses forward.

Chapter 7:

Sara Blakely –Quick Choices in Entrepreneurship

Sara Blakely, founder of Spanx, built her billion-dollar empire by acting fast. She took decisive steps, like launching her prototype without waiting for approval.

Case Study: Data-Driven Decision-Making in Business

Source: Analyst Journey

This study examines the rapid decision-making strategies employed by Netflix and Amazon, demonstrating that swift, informed choices can lead to long-term success.

Key Takeaway: Fast decisions in uncertain environments create momentum, turning small ideas into major successes.

Chapter 7:

Emergency Responders & Athletes—High-Stakes Decisions

First Responders: Paramedics, firefighters, and military personnel rely on split-second judgment to save lives. Studies show that instinctive responses often outperform delayed analytical thinking under pressure.

Athletes: Elite competitors must make instant strategic decisions during matches. Research on performance psychology confirms that trusting one's instincts boosts accuracy and yields better results in sports.

📖 Case Study: Decision-Making Under Pressure

🔍 Source: National Center for Performance Psychology

Examining how emergency responders make rapid decisions under stress, this study highlights the importance of decisive action in high-risk situations.

💡 Key Takeaway: Fast, instinctive choices are critical in high-stakes professions.

Chapter 7:

Section 2:

Personal Growth—Overcoming Fear & Hesitation

The Woman Who Reinvented Herself

A professional stuck in a stagnant career spent years overthinking her next move—until she applied the 15-Second Rule. By making a career pivot within seconds, she transitioned into a new industry, found fulfillment, and doubled her income.

☐ Case Study: The Psychology Behind Hesitation

🔍 Source: Psychologs Magazine

This study examines how fear and cognitive biases contribute to hesitation and how structured exercises can enhance confidence.

Key Takeaway: Hesitation keeps people trapped. Fast decisions create momentum.

Variations for Different Personality Types

- ✓ Not everyone makes decisions in the same way. Here is how to tailor the 15-Second Rule based on individual traits:
- ✓ Analytical Thinkers – Structure decisions by identifying clear options and choosing quickly within a set framework.
- ✓ Intuitive Decision-Makers – Reinforce gut-based choices with confidence exercises.
- ✓ Risk-Averse Individuals – Minimize fear by framing quick decisions as low-stakes experiments rather than irreversible commitments.

Chapter 7:

Progress Tracking Template

Encouraging daily use of this template reinforces habit formation and demonstrates how quick decision-making reduces hesitation over time.

Date			
Decisions			
Time Taken (15 sec max)			
Did hesitation occur? (Yes/No)			
Confidence Level (1-10)			
Outcome & Insights			

Final Thought: Learning to Trust Quick Decisions

Across business, entrepreneurship, and personal growth, hesitation is the most significant barrier to success. The 15-Second Rule empowers people to break free from doubt, act decisively, and move forward with confidence. With research-backed insights and practical applications, making fast decisions is key to unlocking personal and professional success.

Chapter 8:

The Path to Mental Freedom

Objective: Show how practicing the 15-Second Rule can create lasting personal transformation, freeing readers from hesitation and overthinking. This chapter will provide a roadmap for integrating the technique into daily life and maintaining long-term mental clarity.

1. How the 15-Second Rule Transforms Your Life

The shift from hesitation to action is more than a habit—it is a mindset change. By consistently applying fast decision-making, you:

- ✓ Reduce stress: Overthinking drains energy. Quick decisions eliminate mental clutter.
- ✓ Build confidence: Trusting your instincts strengthens self-assurance.
- ✓ Create momentum: Decisiveness keeps you moving forward instead of getting stuck in doubt.

Individuals who adopt the 15-Second Rule experience immediate improvements in their productivity, relationships, and emotional wellbeing. What begins as a simple exercise turns into a fundamental shift in thinking.

Chapter 8:

2. Overcoming the Fear of Making the Wrong Choice

One of the most significant barriers to fast decision-making is the fear of making mistakes. But hesitation is the real enemy, not the mistake itself.

+ Fact: Most decisions, big or small, can be adjusted or course-corrected. The key is movement, not perfection.

+ Mindset Shift: Instead of obsessing over the "best" choice, focus on making a good enough choice quickly and refining it later if needed.

3. The Next Steps for Personal Growth

Mastering the 15-Second Rule is just the beginning. Here is how to keep building momentum in everyday life:

Daily Application Plan

☑ Morning Decisions: Train your brain to start the day without hesitation—what to wear, what task to tackle first.

☑ Work & Career: Stop second-guessing emails, proposals, or meetings—take action without dwelling too long.

☑ Social Life: Practice responding with confidence in conversations without overanalyzing interactions.

Tracking Progress: Keep a journal for one month, noting situations where the 15-Second Rule helped you act decisively.

Chapter 8:

Final Thought: Mental Freedom Starts with Action

Hesitation keeps us trapped. Making fast, confident choices frees the mind and allows you to live with clarity and momentum. The more you practice, the more natural it becomes—and soon, overthinking will no longer hold you back.

Conclusion

Hesitation is a silent thief. It robs you of opportunities, delays progress, and keeps you trapped in a cycle of hesitation. But it does not have to—because every Decision you make is a chance to take control.

Think about the moments in your life where everything could have changed—if only you had acted quicker. How many times have you waited too long, hoping and expecting things to work out on their own? Staying still with absolute certainty, only to watch the moment slip away? The truth is nothing happens on its own.

My father always told me, "Help yourself, and I will help you." It stuck with me, though I never fully understood it—until it hit me. Wanting something is not enough. You must work for it. If you fight for something long enough, giving that final push—the help you have been praying for—will arrive. To succeed, you cannot stay still. You have to break through inertia. Take matters into your hands, the most important step is the first.

The 15-Second Rule is not about making faster decisions. It is about reshaping your mindset. It rewires your brain to trust yourself, embrace the unknown, and take action without letting fear dictate your choices.

Conclusion

Imagine a world where doubt does not hold you back, where opportunities are not wasted on hesitation. Where you step into new experiences with confidence and clarity, knowing that every choice—big or small—moves you toward growth.

Life is a constant evolution, and change is not just inevitable—it's essential. The best way to truly experience life is through freedom, unburdened by doubt and hesitation.

Stop second-guessing yourself. Failure isn't the end—it's part of learning and growth. And the beauty of it all? It only takes 15 seconds to move from where you are to someplace you've never been. A single moment of courage can redefine everything.

Embrace the power of fast decisions. Let go of fear. Step forward.

The world is waiting.

References & Further Reading

Books & Academic Sources

- Kahneman, Daniel. *Thinking, Fast and Slow*. Farrar, Straus, and Giroux, 2011.

- Schwartz, Barry. *The Paradox of Choice: Why More is Less*. HarperCollins, 2004.

- Heath, Chip & Heath, Dan. *Decisive: How to Make Better Choices in Life and Work*. Crown Business, 2013.

Articles & Research Studies

- "Decide with Confidence: Simple Steps to Overcome Indecision" – MentalZon

- "4 Steps to Overcoming Hesitation" – Complete Wellbeing

- "Why Do We Try to Dodge Difficult Decisions?" – Innovative Human Capital

Case Studies

- "The Hidden Costs of Hesitation in Startups" – FasterCapital

- "The Psychology Behind Hesitation" – Psychologs Magazine

www.ingramcontent.com/pod-product-compliance
Lightning Source LLC
Chambersburg PA
CBHW060543030426
42337CB00021B/4414